<u>United States</u> <u>Presidents</u>

William Taft

<u>Paul Joseph</u>
ABDO Publishing Company

visit us at
www.abdopub.com

Published by Abdo Publishing Company, 4940 Viking Drive, Edina, Minnesota 55435. Copyright © 2001 by Abdo Consulting Group, Inc. International copyrights reserved in all countries. No part of this book may be reproduced in any form without written permission from the publisher.

Printed in the United States.

Photo Credits: A/P Wide World, Corbis, William Howard Taft National Historic Site

Contributing editors: Bob Italia, Kate A. Furlong, Christine Phillips
Book design/maps: Patrick Laurel

Library of Congress Cataloging-in-Publication Data

Joseph, Paul, 1970-
　　William Taft / by Paul Joseph.
　　　　p.　cm. -- (United States presidents)
　　Includes index.
　　Summary: Examines the private life and political career of the only president who also served as chief justice of the Supreme Court.
　　ISBN 1-57765-300-9
　　1. Taft, William H. (William Howard), 1857-1930--Juvenile literature.
　　2. Presidents--United States--Biography--Juvenile literature.
　　[1. Taft, William H. (William Howard), 1857-1930. 2. Presidents.]　I. Title.
　　II. Series: United States presidents (Edina, Minn.)
　　E762.J67　1999
　　973.91'2'092--dc21
　　[B]　　　　　　　　　　　　　　　　　　　　　　98-22789
　　　　　　　　　　　　　　　　　　　　　　　　　　　CIP
　　　　　　　　　　　　　　　　　　　　　　　　　　　AC

Contents

William Taft

William Taft was the twenty-seventh president of the United States. He was also **chief justice** of the **Supreme Court**. Taft is the only person in U.S. history to hold both offices.

Taft came from a wealthy family. They helped him get a good education. Taft attended Yale University and the Cincinnati Law School.

Taft worked as a lawyer and a judge. Later, he served as governor of the Philippines. He also worked as **secretary of war** under President Theodore Roosevelt.

In 1908, Americans elected Taft president. He broke up **trusts**. And he worked to lower **tariffs**. During this time, the **Republican** party was divided. Taft tried to work with both sides of the party. But they could not get along.

Taft lost the next election to Woodrow Wilson. After leaving the White House, Taft became a professor at Yale. Then he served as chief justice of the Supreme Court. He died in 1930.

President William Taft

William Taft (1857-1930)
Twenty-seventh President

BORN:	September 15, 1857
PLACE OF BIRTH:	Cincinnati, Ohio
ANCESTRY:	English, Scots-Irish
FATHER:	Alphonso Taft (1810-1891)
MOTHER:	Louise Torrey Taft (1827-1907)
WIFE:	Helen "Nellie" Herron (1861-1943)
CHILDREN:	Robert, Helen, Charles
EDUCATION:	Yale University, Cincinnati Law School
RELIGION:	Unitarian
OCCUPATION:	Lawyer, writer, professor
MILITARY SERVICE:	None
POLITICAL PARTY:	Republican

OFFICES HELD:	Assistant prosecutor in Hamilton County, Ohio; collector of internal revenue; judge on Ohio Superior Court; U.S. solicitor general; judge on U.S. Sixth Circuit Court of Appeals; governor of the Philippines; secretary of war; chief justice of the U.S. Supreme Court
AGE AT INAUGURATION:	51
YEARS SERVED:	1909-1913
VICE PRESIDENT:	James S. Sherman
DIED:	March 8, 1930, in Washington, D.C., age 72
CAUSE OF DEATH:	Heart disease

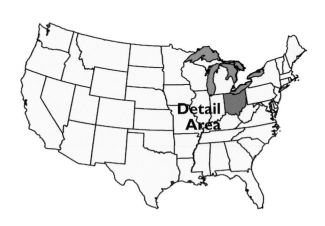

Birthplace of William Taft

Young Will

William Howard Taft was born in Cincinnati, Ohio, on September 15, 1857. Everyone called him Will. Will's parents were Louise and Alphonso Taft. Alphonso was a successful lawyer. He also served in President Grant's **cabinet**.

The Taft family was large. Will had two brothers, Henry and Horace. He also had one sister, Fanny. And he had two half-brothers, Charles and Peter.

Young Will attended local schools. But school was not easy for him. He had to study hard. His classmates teased him about this. They also teased him because he was big. They called him "Lubber." Despite the teasing, Will had many friends.

In 1874, Will graduated from high school. Then he attended Yale University in New Haven, Connecticut. He studied hard. He also played football, rowed, and boxed. In 1878, Will graduated. All his hard studying paid off. He was ranked second in his class.

Will Taft (front row, center) with his high school classmates in 1874

Work & Family

*A*fter graduating from Yale, Taft decided to be a lawyer. He attended Cincinnati Law School. Taft graduated in 1880. Then he worked at his father's law office.

In 1881, Taft became an assistant **prosecuting attorney** in Hamilton County, Ohio. He also worked for a short time as Cincinnati's collector of **internal revenue**.

In 1884, Taft began dating Helen "Nellie" Herron. She was the daughter of a well-known lawyer. William and Nellie got married in 1886. They had three children named Robert, Helen, and Charles.

Taft became a judge on the Ohio Superior Court in 1887. He greatly enjoyed his work. He hoped to one day become a **Supreme Court justice**.

In 1890, President Harrison asked Taft to be the new U.S. solicitor general. Taft accepted. The job allowed him to argue cases before the Supreme Court.

Two years later, Taft took a new job. He served as a judge on the U.S. Sixth Circuit Court of Appeals. He kept this job for eight years. During this time, he was also **dean** of the Cincinnati Law School.

The Taft Family: (front row) Robert, Charles, and Helen; (back row) William and Nellie

Governor Taft

*I*n 1898, the Philippine Islands became a U.S. territory. In 1900, President McKinley sent Taft there to establish order and form a government. The next year, Taft became the first **civil** governor of the Philippines.

Taft developed a court system. He built roads, harbors, and schools. He worked for land **reforms** and an improved **economy**. And he hoped that one day the Filipinos would run their own government. But independence would not come until 1946.

The Tafts enjoyed the Philippines. They lived on a large estate with servants. They held many dinners, parties, and balls.

In 1902, President Roosevelt asked Taft to be a **justice** on the **Supreme Court**. Taft had always wanted this job. But he did not take it. He felt his work in the Philippines was unfinished.

The Filipinos did not want Taft to leave, either. They approved of his gentle leadership. And Nellie was happy with her grand life on the islands.

In 1903, President Roosevelt asked Taft to be his **secretary of war**. Nellie encouraged Taft to take the job. But Taft was unsure if he was right for the job. And he had "no love for American politics." But Roosevelt finally convinced Taft to join his **cabinet**.

Detail Area

SOUTHEAST ASIA

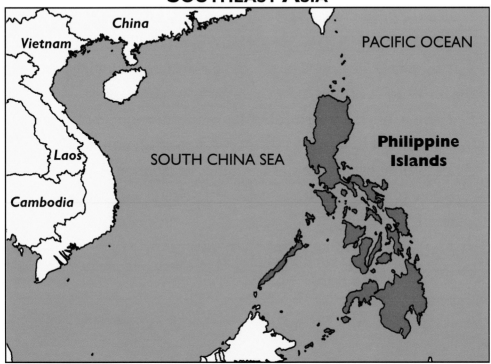

Secretary Taft

*I*n 1904, Taft returned to Washington, D.C., to become **secretary of war**. He oversaw the construction of the **Panama Canal**. And he set up the government in the Canal Zone.

Roosevelt and Taft worked well together. Roosevelt often assigned Taft special tasks. For example, Taft helped Roosevelt work on the Treaty of Portsmouth. It ended the **Russo-Japanese War** in 1905.

Roosevelt announced he would not seek re-election in 1908. He recommended Taft as the **Republican** candidate. At first, Taft objected. He hoped to join the **Supreme Court** instead. But Taft's wife and brothers changed his mind.

Taft easily won the Republican **nomination**. James S. Sherman was chosen as his vice president. Taft defeated **Democrat** William Jennings Bryan in the election.

Opposite page: Taft (right) walks alongside railroad tracks while inspecting the Panama Canal.

The Making of the Twenty-seventh United States President

 **1857**

Born
September 15
in Cincinnati,
Ohio

 **1878**

Graduates from
Yale University

 **1880**

Graduates
from
Cincinnati
Law School

 **1887**

Becomes a
judge on Ohio
Superior Court

 **1890**

Becomes the
U.S. solicitor
general

 **1892**

Serves as federal
judge and dean of
Cincinnati Law
School

 **1904**

Serves as
President
Roosevelt's
secretary of
war

1908

Elected
president of
the United
States

1909

Payne-Aldrich
Tariff Act
becomes law

1912

Arizona and New
Mexico become states;
Taft loses election to
Woodrow Wilson

PRESIDENTIAL   YEARS

William Taft

"I am afraid I am a constant disappointment to my party. The fact of the matter is, the longer I am president, the less of a party man I seem to become."

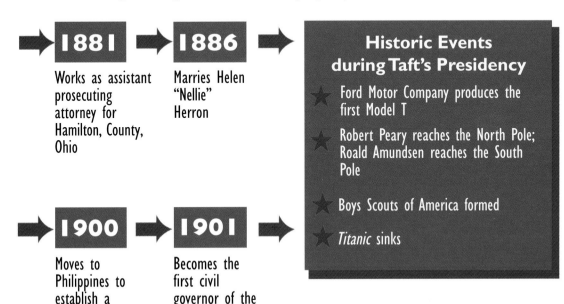

1881
Works as assistant prosecuting attorney for Hamilton, County, Ohio

1886
Marries Helen "Nellie" Herron

Historic Events during Taft's Presidency

★ Ford Motor Company produces the first Model T

★ Robert Peary reaches the North Pole; Roald Amundsen reaches the South Pole

★ Boys Scouts of America formed

★ *Titanic* sinks

1900
Moves to Philippines to establish a government

1901
Becomes the first civil governor of the Philippines

1913
Leaves the White House; becomes a law professor at Yale University

1921
Becomes chief justice of the Supreme Court

1930
Dies on March 8

President Taft

*T*aft took office in March 1909. He had doubts about being president. He knew he could not be another Roosevelt. "Our ways are different," he said. Taft wanted to take Roosevelt's ideas and make them better.

But Taft had trouble from the start. The **Republican** party soon became divided.

Taft wanted **Congress** to lower **tariffs**. The **House of Representatives** had many **liberal** Republicans. They quickly passed a bill sponsored by Sereno E. Payne. It lowered many tariffs.

Then the bill went to the **Senate**. Senator Nelson W. Aldrich made many changes to the bill. His changes kept several important tariffs very high.

President Taft signed the Payne-Aldrich Tariff Act into law in 1909. The law did not lower as many tariffs as Taft had promised.

Taft accepted the law and justified it in public. But the law angered **liberal Republicans**. And many Americans felt President Taft had gone back on his word.

Presidents Theodore Roosevelt and William Taft

Taft had more party trouble in 1909. Gifford Pinchot was the country's **chief forester**. He said that Richard Ballinger, the **secretary of the interior**, had made dishonest land deals. But Taft believed Ballinger was innocent. A special group of Congressmen cleared Ballinger's name. Then Taft fired Pinchot.

Gifford Pinchot

Liberal Republicans believed Pinchot. They grew unhappy with Taft. They began to turn to Roosevelt as their true leader.

Despite his troubles with Republicans, Taft had some success with **Congress**. He helped form the **Tariff Board** and the Federal Children's Bureau. He took the first steps toward establishing a **federal budget**.

Taft also wanted to require candidates to publish campaign expenses in federal elections. Taft broke up many **trusts**. In 1912, he made Arizona and New Mexico U.S. states. And he made Alaska a U.S. territory.

THE UNITED STATES DURING TAFT'S PRESIDENCY

Existing States

New States

New Territory

Helen Taft

While Taft was president, his wife had a stroke. She was too sick to be a hostess at the White House. So young Helen Taft often took her place. Taft missed his wife's help after she became ill. He had relied on her keen political advice.

In 1910, Roosevelt began making many **liberal** speeches. He talked about a "New Nationalism." He stood for honest government, social justice, and increased **welfare**.

Roosevelt's speeches upset many **conservative Republicans**. They lined up with Taft against Roosevelt. The Republican party had split in two. Conservative Republicans supported Taft. Liberal Republicans supported Roosevelt.

In 1912, conservative Republicans **renominated** Taft for president. Roosevelt and the liberal Republicans refused to lose. They organized the **Progressive** party and nominated Roosevelt for president.

A newspaper reporter asked Roosevelt how he felt about his election chances. Roosevelt replied, "as strong as a bull moose." The new party was soon nicknamed the Bull Moose party.

The **Democratic** party **nominated** Governor Woodrow Wilson of New Jersey. With the **Republican** party split in two, it had little power. So Wilson easily won the election.

Taft gives a campaign speech in 1912.

The Seven "Hats" of the U.S. President

To be president, a person must have lived in the country for at least 14 years, must be a U.S. citizen born in America, and must be at least 35 years old.

A president is elected or re-elected every four years.

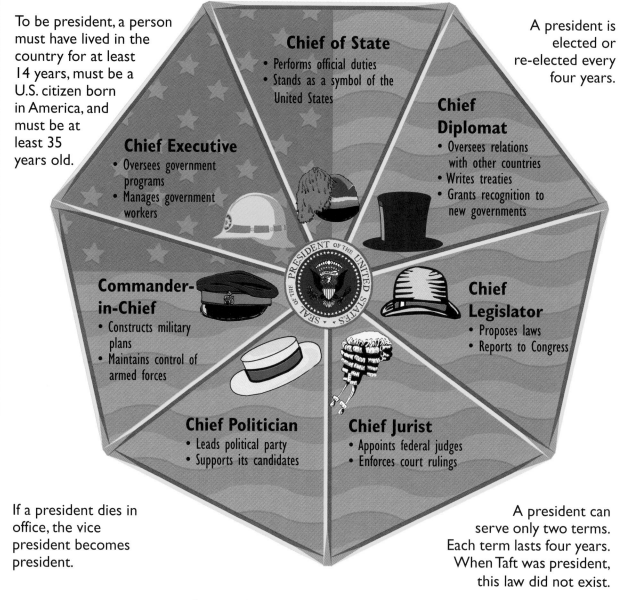

Chief of State
- Performs official duties
- Stands as a symbol of the United States

Chief Diplomat
- Oversees relations with other countries
- Writes treaties
- Grants recognition to new governments

Chief Executive
- Oversees government programs
- Manages government workers

Commander-in-Chief
- Constructs military plans
- Maintains control of armed forces

Chief Legislator
- Proposes laws
- Reports to Congress

Chief Politician
- Leads political party
- Supports its candidates

Chief Jurist
- Appoints federal judges
- Enforces court rulings

If a president dies in office, the vice president becomes president.

A president can serve only two terms. Each term lasts four years. When Taft was president, this law did not exist.

As president, William Taft had seven jobs.

The Three Branches of the U.S. Government

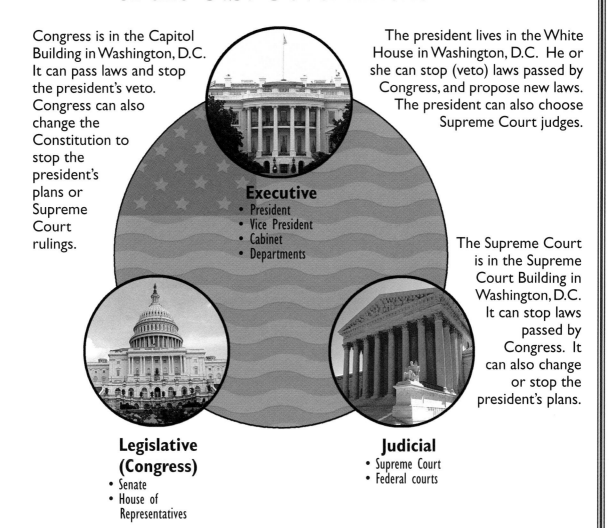

Congress is in the Capitol Building in Washington, D.C. It can pass laws and stop the president's veto. Congress can also change the Constitution to stop the president's plans or Supreme Court rulings.

The president lives in the White House in Washington, D.C. He or she can stop (veto) laws passed by Congress, and propose new laws. The president can also choose Supreme Court judges.

Executive
- President
- Vice President
- Cabinet
- Departments

The Supreme Court is in the Supreme Court Building in Washington, D.C. It can stop laws passed by Congress. It can also change or stop the president's plans.

Legislative (Congress)
- Senate
- House of Representatives

Judicial
- Supreme Court
- Federal courts

The U.S. Constitution formed three government branches. Each branch has power over the others. So no single group or person can control the country. The Constitution calls this "separation of powers."

Chief Justice

*T*aft left the White House in 1913. He became a law professor at Yale. He continued to follow politics in Washington, D.C. And he traveled across the nation giving speeches.

America entered **World War I** in 1917. The next year, Taft helped lead the National War Labor Board. It improved relations between American businesses and their workers. This increased the production of goods, which helped win the war.

In 1921, President Harding asked Taft to be **chief justice** of the **Supreme Court**. Taft accepted. He is the only president to hold this job.

The Supreme Court was overloaded with cases. So Taft asked **Congress** to pass the Judges Bill. It would give the Supreme Court more freedom in choosing its cases. This would get rid of backed-up cases and let the court run smoothly. Congress passed the Judges Bill in 1925.

Chief Justice Taft did other important work, too. He helped win approval for a new **Supreme Court** building. It is still used today. Taft also wrote **opinions** on 253 cases.

In February 1930, Taft retired from the Supreme Court. He died of heart problems a month later. Taft was buried in Arlington National Cemetery in Virginia.

As president, Taft wanted to lower **tariffs**, end **trusts**, and establish a **federal budget**. He was successful with many of these projects. But Taft's time in office was marked by fighting within the **Republican** party. This greatly weakened Taft's power as president.

Chief Justice Taft

Fast Facts

- William Taft was the first U.S. president to have a fleet of automobiles.

- William Taft started the tradition of the president throwing out the first ball to open the Major League Baseball season.

- After Nellie Taft traveled to Japan, the mayor of Tokyo sent her three thousand cherry trees. She planted the first one herself. Today, the cherry blossoms are a well-known attraction in Washington, D.C.

- Taft was the last president to keep a cow on the White House lawn. The cow was called Pauline Wayne. She supplied the milk that was served at the White House table.

William and Nellie Taft ride in the first presidential automobile.

Glossary

cabinet - a group of advisers chosen by the president.

chief forester - the person in charge of the U.S. Forest Service.

chief justice - the head judge of the Supreme Court.

civil - not connected with the church or the military.

Congress - the lawmaking body of the U.S. It is made up of the Senate and the House of Representatives. It meets in Washington, D.C.

conservative - a person who has traditional beliefs and often dislikes change.

dean - a person at a university who is in charge of discipline, activities, studies, and guidance of students.

Democrat - a political party that is liberal and believes in big government.

economy - the way a state or nation uses its money, goods, and natural resources.

federal budget - a plan showing how the national government's money will be spent during a certain period of time.

House of Representatives - the lower house in the U.S. Congress. Citizens elect members of the house to make laws for the nation.

internal revenue - the income a government collects from its citizens and puts to use in public projects.

justice - a judge on the Supreme Court.

liberal - a person who favors changes and progress.

nominate - to name a person as a candidate for office. If a person is nominated for another term in office, he or she has been renominated.

opinion - a legal explanation of a judge's decision on a particular case.

Panama Canal - a narrow canal in Panama that connects the Atlantic and Pacific Oceans.

Progressive - a political party that split from the Republican party around 1912. Also known as the Bull Moose party.

prosecuting attorney - a lawyer who represents the government in criminal cases.

reform - to make a change for the better.

Republican - a political party that is conservative and believes in small government.

Russo-Japanese War - a war between Russia and Japan that began in 1904. They fought for control of Korea and Manchuria. The war ended with the Treaty of Portsmouth in 1905.

secretary of the interior - the person in charge of the Department of the Interior. This department manages public lands and protects wildlife.

secretary of war - an adviser to the president who handles the nation's defense.

Senate - the upper house in the U.S. Congress. Citizens elect senators to make laws for the nation.

Supreme Court - the highest, most powerful court in the United States.

tariffs - fees or taxes placed on goods from foreign countries.

trust - a business that illegally controls a certain good or service, which stops competition.

welfare - money that the government gives to people in need.

World War I - 1914 to 1918, fought in Europe. The United States, Great Britain, France, Russia, and their allies were on one side. Germany, Austria-Hungary, and their allies were on the other side. The war began when Archduke Ferdinand of Austria was assassinated. America joined the war in 1917 because Germany began attacking ships that weren't involved in the war.

Internet Sites

The Presidents of the United States of America
http://www.whitehouse.gov/WH/glimpse/presidents/html/presidents.html
Part of the White House Web site.

William Howard Taft's Boyhood Home
http://www.cr.nps.gov/nr/twhp/wwwlps/lessons/15taft.htm
Part of the National Parks Web site.

These sites are subject to change. Go to your favorite search engine and type in "United States Presidents" for more sites.

Index